EX LIBRIS

"WHO GIVES?
WHO RECEIVES?
IN THE GIFT MOMENT
ONLY TWO HANDS IN
EXCHANGE."

JUDITH LEE STRONACH
25 MAY 1943
29 NOVEMBER 2002
STONEWALL

THE OTHER SIDE OF THE HILL
1975 - 1995

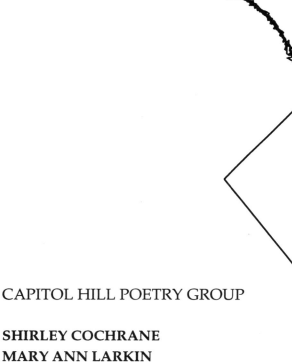

CAPITOL HILL POETRY GROUP

SHIRLEY COCHRANE
MARY ANN LARKIN
CHRIS LLEWELLYN
JEAN NORDHAUS
PATRIC PEPPER
ROBERT SARGENT
ELIZABETH SULLAM
KEITH YANCY
EDWIN ZIMMERMAN

THE OTHER SIDE OF THE HILL

1975 - 1995

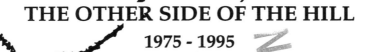
Forest Woods Media Productions Inc.
Washington, D.C.

International Standard Book Number: 0-938572-18-0
Library of Congress Card Number: 96-085462
First Edition published in the U.S.A.

Original cover design by Clarissa Wittenberg
(from first book, *The Other Side of the Hill*, © 1979)

Cover revision and book typography by
Cindy Comitz, *In Support* Graphics

Printing by George Klear, *Printing Press, Inc.*

Book orders:
The Writer's Center
4508 Walsh Avenue
Bethesda, Maryland 20815

Forest Woods Media Productions Inc.
The Bunny and the Crocodile Press
Washington, D.C.

ACKNOWLEDGMENTS

SHIRLEY COCHRANE: "Answer" was first published in *Potato Eyes*; "The Route of Eli Washington" in her book, *Families & Other Strangers* (Washington, D.C.: Word Works).

MARY ANN LARKIN: "August Days" has appeared in *Lip Service*.

CHRIS LLEWELLYN: "At Rest in Greenwood" was first published in her book, *Fragments from the Fire: the Triangle Shirtwaist Company Fire of March 25, 1911* (Viking Penguin Books, Inc.—winner of the Walt Whitman Award for 1986); "The Cairo Hotel" in *Who Is My Neighbor?...a Study Guide from the Editors of Sojourners*.

JEAN NORDHAUS: "Illustrations" was first published in *New Republic*; "Drink" in *Ruby*; "The White Meal" in *West Branch* and reprinted in *Quarterly Review of Literature Anthology*.

PATRIC PEPPER: "The Truck Driver's Husband: a Letter" and "Words for Weldon" first appeared, in earlier versions, in *Poetpourri*.

ROBERT SARGENT: "The Piano Seat Cover" first appeared in *Pembroke Magazine*; "The Things of the World" in *Poetry*; "Young Man Away from Home" in *Hollins Critic*; "Tin Roof Blues" in *The Jazz Poetry Anthology* (Indiana University Press); "Faulkner" in *Negative Capability*; "Trimeters" in *Poetry East*.

KEITH YANCY: "Legend" and "A Good Day in a Bad Neighborhood," first appeared in *Obsidian 2*; "Legend" was also published in *The African-American Review*.

EDWIN ZIMMERMAN: "Dido Was Smitten" first appeared in *Partisan Review*.

PREFACE

The Capitol Hill Poetry Group came about as
much by accident as by design. It was 1975, a time of
many beginnings. Jean Nordhaus, who was just
beginning to write poetry, went to Sally Crowell,
founder of the new Capitol Hill Arts Workshop,
looking for a poetry workshop. Sally told her how to
track down a woman named Shirley Cochrane who'd
inquired about just such a workshop. Jean found
Shirley in a carrel in the main reading room at the
Library of Congress. They talked and agreed to
begin meeting together.

The first gatherings of the still unnamed group
took place in a Sunday School room of the Capitol
Hill Presbyterian Church. The new members re-
cruited by Jean and Shirley squatted on pint-sized
chairs by low tables to nervously share poems. The
first tentative ways of working together began to
emerge. Shortly the group graduated to adult-sized
chairs in their own living rooms where they have
been bringing poems to each other weekly, or mostly
so, ever since.

Within a few years, the group coalesced into "a
poetic family," as Peter Petcoff dubbed us. From that
first cohesive group, which lasted until 1982, Jean
and Shirley, Mary Ann Larkin and Chris Llewellyn
remain, while Cary McKee, Gray Jacobik, Hastings
Wyman, Jr., and Russell Spicer have moved on.
Also, that same year, with the death of Peter Petcoff,
who had for many years been reference librarian at
the Library of Congress, the group lost a radiant
spirit as well as a learned critic and loving friend. It
was Peter who had in 1979 named not only the group

but our first anthology, *The Other Side of the Hill*. We agreed the name should identify us as a nonpolitical voice in this most political of cities. The name also stood, and stands even more so today, as a vote for the imaginative life, for the small, personal human voice in a world where, to use poet Robert Hayden's phrase "...monsters of abstraction/ ...threaten us."

After a time of comings and goings, the group again stabilized over the next five years with the arrival of poets Patric Pepper, Elizabeth Sullam, Ed Zimmerman, Keith Yancy and Robert Sargent to its present nine members. Throughout these changes over two decades, our ethos and way of working has remained constant: absolute honesty coupled with respect both for the person and the poem. We believe in language as a way of both shaping and revealing the world—the other side of the hill.

Now it has been 20 years. The passing time has brought us weddings, births—and many books of poems by our members. We are older, perhaps wiser. We meet earlier and drink less wine, but we still laugh and gossip and eat until the cry "Let's do poetry" puts us to work. Our lives and poems have changed, been made far richer over these 20 years, as together we've made a space for the imagination. And so with this second collection, we invite you to the other side of the hill, hoping that these poems will give you as much pleasure in the reading as they gave us in the making.

—The Capitol Hill Poetry Group

CONTENTS

I

If Love's a Puzzle

The Piano Seat Cover

Something she did, insisted on, those last days,
was to make, embroider, a piano seat cover for Bob,
my son by a former marriage, whom she'd come
to love as her son, too. Something to leave him.

Propped up in bed with pillows, she sewed for hours
a colorful design. He didn't know about this,
living in another city, waiting to be called.
Toward the end she saw she couldn't make it,

the design was botched a little, unsteady fingers.
She picked at it with her needle, trying to fix it,
then gave me firm instructions what to do:
take it to a certain seamstress for completion.

These days when I visit my son, I wait until
no one is near, and go to the piano seat
and look for, discover, the picked-at small blemish
she'd left on the cover. Her fingers there once, trying.

Robert Sargent

Valentines

(Catherine and Douglas Valentine)

The broom-maker and his wife,
both blind, carried their craft
from door to door. In Sunday best
he stroked the straws to show
how carefully he counted, then
bound them in a strong red cord.
She'd ruffle his besoms of sorghum
twigs—stiff and rough enough to
sweep out gutter spouts or
hearthstones. Her blue, wide eyes
had never seen, and his, child–
sized, stayed closed under
a shock of brown hair. Are lights
shut off, paper shades drawn down
in their two room nest downtown?
In one, poles and panicles
wait in particular places, while
in another the iron bedstead,
fragrant with broomcorn and sawdust,
strums its tuneful harpstrings
into their moonstruck darkness.

Chris Llewellyn

Chagall's *The Rooster*

Here as in a dream her deep delight,
So deep she doesn't smile but stares to space
In painted light that drapes a field in lace,
Is to lay her only body on his bright

And feathered form, hot as a meteorite.
Chagall has painted them in red: red face,
Red crop, red hair. She rides that bird, her grace
The rooster's dance throughout the lavender night.

Late love? Young heat? Chagall, perhaps, would know.
Off on his lake some other lovers drift
In bluish light where full they hold each other.

We gaze at paint, but feel the give and glow;
If love's a puzzle, here the pieces fit.
Dance! Dance now cheek to beak! O, ride him, lover!

Patric Pepper

Sabbath Eve

They say the pious Sephardic woman, knowing
The Law commands a husband to make love
To his wife on Friday nights, will cook a meal
Contrived to warm his appetite. I almost see
The newly-scrubbed and spotless Sabbath house,
The clean white tablecloths, the braided bread,
Brass candelabra burnished to gold,
The serene flame of twice-blessed candles,
As he enters after prayers, having worshipped
As he should, wearing best shirt, best suit,
The long, quiet Sabbath Saturday
Stretching ahead, and sits at the table
Of his dark-eyed, dark-haired wife
Who quietly says: Eat, eat.

Edwin Zimmerman

The Truck Driver's Husband: A Letter

after Ezra Pound, after Rihaku (Li Tai Po)

While Mom was still cropping me crew cut close,
I played around the trailer park, in jeans
And hot rod tee shirts, vandalizing all.
You used to swing by—swing your girlish hips—
Smack your red lips off cherry Popsicles,
And say that I could just whip the weenie
Forever. So we plagued that crazy place,
Taunting the neighbors, pissed on and pissed off.

At sixteen we married. You were pregnant.
I never laughed for years, being frightened,
But hired on at Smitty's Gulf for peanuts.
I pumped gas, changed oil. I learned to fix cars.
When you'd come down with Danny on your hip,
I wouldn't look up from under the hood.

At twenty-six I wanted you forever.
Never sorry then, I stared away,
Dreamed of the place I'd have with you, the home
Where I would die someday and be carried out.

At thirty-eight, you got your license. You left
To drive a rig from Florida to Maine.
And you've been gone ten months. The semis
Winding out at night—I think and think.

I'm sober five months and painted the house.
I wish that you could see the garden this year.
We've four bushels of beans, tons of tomatoes.
It hurts me. I'm sorry. My beard is peppered.
If you swing past and have time to talk, please
Call me beforehand and I will meet you
Anywhere you like on I-95.

Patric Pepper

Katama

Off Katama the Atlantic
was sparkling like Wampanoag
turquoise.

Under a crystal sun
I watched my skin turn
to copper, my lips to plums.

She is still an enigma
to me after nineteen years
the woman who comes to the beach

wearing a new bathing suit
of lemon cream but does not enter
the minty waters.

She wants only to read
Mary Higgins Clark on a blanket
woven of sky and sunshowers

and to hear her mantra sung
by surf and sand. I fell in
love with her all over again.

Keith Yancy

Ascension

Love lures life on.
—Thomas Hardy

Now somehow out of the dark earth they rise:
Venus, the moon—no distant galaxy.
They cannot match the caring in your eyes.

About the yard the crickets chirp—unwise,
Untutored tunes of rankest purity;
As somehow out of the dark earth they rise.

Soon we'll stand in stars, in blazing skies
Of vast incertitude, bright neutrality;
What can match the caring in your eyes,

Or how around your pond all colonize,
Freewheeling creatures of starred infinity?
Somehow out of the dark earth they rise.

Tomorrow the stolid sun will trim the guise
Of redwings guarding marshland territory;
They will not match the caring in your eyes.

Tonight we'll sleep together, in dream devise
The way we coalesce to care completely.
Somehow, out of the dark earth we rise;
I live to match the caring in your eyes.

Patric Pepper

Dido Was Smitten

Dido was smitten by that great dolt Aeneas.
She did not know why. Perhaps
It was the bronze helmet with bristling arc
Of horsehair, or his gleaming pectorals,
Or the dark bass intoning the fall of Troy,
Or the squat broadsword dangling at his side.
She was smitten but he was not
And the gifts she gave he later gave away,
Placating some lesser god or goddess
Or dressing the corpse of a secondary hero
With robes she had woven, embroidered with silver,
Forgetting, if he ever knew, how she had looked
When they went hunting, a quiver at her back,
Her short cloak caught around her shoulders,
Her hair tied up with gold and a brooch of gold
Pinning her scarlet dress as she moved like a doe
With an arrow in her that was not yet felt.

Edwin Zimmerman

Illustrations

I knew the rudiments: his
into hers. What I lacked
were illustrations. My parents
handed me a solemn book.
It would explain
what they could not. Feverish,
I browsed the chapters ("Eggs,"
"Pollen and Sperm"),
past grainy fish roe
(black and white); a nest
of speckled eggs, a flustered
German Shepherd bitch
who nursed her puppies
like the Roman she-wolf
standing up. All this
I took for metaphor.
Likewise, the sad
fallopian lyre, the bristling
snapdragons, the peacock's
gorgeous poker-hand of plumes.
Only to reach the final
chapter, where an uxorious
bull and cow moose browsed
in a soggy glade, fondling
the ferns with blowzy lips. And *this*,
it seemed, was frenzy's end: the bog,
the weeds, the slow beasts
cumbrous in their bodies.

Jean Nordhaus

Bulls

The farmer down the road put two
Black Angus bulls into my pasture
Where they were in residence for a month.
Big as freight cars, shoulders bursting,
With black ballocks the size of soccer balls
And complex pouches hanging underneath
From which a pizzle red as a torch
Forayed from time to time, they vacuumed up
The grass and sometimes tried to hump each other
But gave up quickly. They were indifferent
To my presence: they waited for but one thing
And I was not it.
They were taken off one afternoon
And in their place nine Black Angus cows
Came to stay, some ready for love.
They wandered about,
Splattered with their own flop
Wearing clouds of flies, sprouting orange
Tags from each ear and wheeling
Like a flock of birds as I walked in their field.
I did not think they were particularly
Attractive. And yet I know those bulls would kill
To be where I was—
Those black haunches! That Paradise!

Edwin Zimmerman

Call My Dog

My baby gone. She walked straight
out our dilapidated door. My baby
gone. When she left I knew she wasn't
coming back here no more. Well, I know
I been real bad, but since she gone
I just seems to feel so sad.

Since she gone, these cold walls can't
seem to comfort me. Since she gone
if me and my hound dog howls, just let us be.
These nights they's so long. Last
midnight we had a fight and he was gone.

Call my dog. I would if I could figure
a way from here. Call my dog. He the only
one don't shame me for my tears. I done
raised him from a pup. We takes our gin
from the same china cup.

If he run, it's cause he thinks I'm still
mad at him today. If he run, it's cause
last midnight he stole my pork pie away.
Well I ain't still mad. That pot missed
his head and I'm so glad.

Call my dog. Send him back down the road.
We won't fight. I got a feeling; it's going
to be a good night for howling tonight.

Keith Yancy

A Young Woman Writes from London

Life in general is not bad except
That London in November is dark and drab,
And I live in a cramped room. When I'm tired
I feel as though I'm floating in a gray sea,
Quite lost, belonging to no one
And to no place, with only tiers of fog
On the horizon. I long for a clean,
Airy house, bright with sunlight,
With high ceilings, banks of flowers, pictures
Coloring the wall, decent furniture
And a fine stereo. And although
None of the males around are suitable
For the purpose, I feel in the mood
For a violent love affair.

Edwin Zimmerman

II

Heaven Cracks and Tatters

Disappearances

"There were estuaries here"—you say—
"A port with classic statues, mosaics.
The mausoleum's dome made of one single
stone remains. Pines, umbrella pines,
wind-bent, bowed to the limpid beach!
The sea and air were odorous with salt
and resins, and if you dived deep, till
your ears burst, you could see columns,
capitals, friezes shimmer on the sea-bed.
Here I dug a small Etruscan bronze, all
sea-green, a boy riding a donkey." You look
at the face of your teenage granddaughter
whose eyes are devouring a blond lifeguard
passing by. "Well," you tell yourself,
"you are no stranger to sudden soliloquies.
BUT THERE WERE ESTUARIES HERE...."

Elizabeth Sullam

Photo of Patric at Nine Years

You were already tall that summer
your bones hiding soft
in your still round face
under flesh soon to stretch
to planes of supple bronze
bone and muscle waiting
in not yet vanished somnolence

Soon, fear and desire
will cleave you in half
as you search for your lost self
in the folds of others' flesh
Reason, too, will tear you
from your boy-self
desperate to know
the hidden shiftings
the cool and singular beauty
of time and matter
Only the unseeing stare
of your dark gold-flecked eyes
even then hoarding gods and stars
will come with you

Summer boy, you knew none of this
and no one could warn you
of yourself coming to claim you
to banish forever
the simple present
of that nine-year-old summer
when you swam
boneless and of a piece

Mary Ann Larkin

At Rest in Greenwood

(Jennie Franco)

My short years wrap me like a cloth
of schooldays, feast days, my First Communion dress.
The cord of mornings, stitching at Triangle
up in the loft before light.

I trace the thread to my last, my fifteenth birthday.
Ribbons of friends dance the Tarantella,
circling plates of tortoni and ices
out on our stoop after dark.

And Mama says, don't forget Our Lady
and always light a holy candle on your birthday.
Today she twists rosary beads between my ruined fingers,
plaits roses in my veil.

Neighbors nail flowers, black crepe
to the doors. They have covered my face
with lilies and forget-me-nots.
I am circled with tapers.

I rest in the front room
next to the room where I was born.
The brass band wraps up our street,
"Panis Angelicus" stops at our stoop.

The Sons of Italy and Saint Angelo Society
have hired a cart just for my flowers.
Papa says, only the best for our Jennie.
A fine lady, I am lifted into my carriage.

The brass-harp of hymns follows the line
of Eleventh Street. Inside its woven voice
I know each murmuring Ave Maria.
The sky smells like lilies.

Slower. Silence. We are nearing Triangle.
Now the shock of the skeleton loft
unfolds the tall wall of wailing till
Heaven cracks and tatters, blesses us with rain.

Chris Llewellyn

The Locket

Your sister's lips quiver in a smile
that belies the moisture in her eyes.
She says, "She wanted you to have it."
For scores of years, hung on a gold chain
around your neck, the locket seemed
a part of your body. My mind hesitates,
but the locket slips through trees,
oceans, rivers, barren hills, plains
to a hellish dawn that found you stunned
in the middle of the hall, your hands
clutching the glorious golden braids
the partisans had cut off. I snap
the locket open to see a lock
of your hair coiled under a yellowish glass.
I distinctly hear Granny's stern voice
rising above cries, "Go along, children!
This is nothing. Hair grows again." And
to you, "Nothing a good wig won't cure.
A small price for a wrong love. Thank God
you came off this mess with your life."
Grandmother and her unshakeable beliefs!
But you and I? For I, who came too late to fetch
you away, to spare you that insult,
the lock of hair is a question mark,
of questions never asked. My fingers
click the lock closed—a fine object
of Florentine workmanship, of love knots
and rings, now in my hand, one of earth's
countless, deciduous things.

Elizabeth Sullam

That Deep and Steady Hum

The Catholics take such good care
of the church of Our Lady
Last Monday just after dawn
the sign man, with furrowed brow
fingered the letters
of Our Lady's name
full of paint chips now
Each week the tiny white-haired lady
carries in the linens
old but crisp and snowy white
while the hedge man cuts
the hedges straight as truth
Familiar and awe-struck as lovers
all of them
even the young artist
who went amuck that winter night
his blue eyes unseeing
and took an ax
to the icons of Our Lady

He came in the dark
with his sweet, blank face
his unsuckled rage
carrying the ax
the way the old woman
carries the linens
feeling the stillness of Our Lady
as the sign man did
when he traced with calloused fingers
her once gilded letters
they to restore
the other
the one with the golden curls
to destroy

And when at last
someone took the ax
and led him away,
his lightning anger
dimming into blankness,
he wept
Shards of her icons
lay splintered on the floor
along with his rage
For what did he know
of great and quiet care
of love pure as milk
of forgiveness
hungry to forgive

Our Lady gathers them all
in her wide arms
the way the bowl of the Dipper
gathers up her steeple
on summer nights
receiving them as she does the tides
holding them in forgiveness—
that deep and steady hum
girdling oceans and moons
and the tiny shrines
we care for and destroy

Mary Ann Larkin

Leaving the Holocaust Museum

Perfection was the pond, a circle cut by the Po
for two youngsters who sat at its smooth edge
unaware that time comes carrying a hatchet.
Living was mostly silence and waiting for the trout
to bite, then biking for ice cream to a shack
just where the river splits into innumerable
inlets before battling the sea,
waiting again until the smoke of dusk plunged
into black velvet night and then biking back
to the dividing poplar line to say "Ciao!
A domani!" And tomorrow, an always
opening future.

Cross and Star, Star and Cross. How
could they know that their dreams—tenuous
Saint Elmo's fires—crawled
out of two separate graveyards?

Was the word love spoken? Were plans made?
Who can think of words which the gelid
northeast wind froze, the madman uttered,
the wild beast and the lamb cried?
Who can lead us back to vanished sites,
roundness of days slipping away?

Still the jar of my memory fills with a hollow
silence. And in that abode of life, for all
who lived, for all whose lives were dispersed
in the spaces of Europe, what is left for the living
is sorrow without sound, like the intake of air
before sobbing. Star and Cross, Cross and Star...

the never-ending story of lives to which,
on earth, grace was not granted, nor the plucking
of a four-leaf clover at the edge of a pond,
that shows the story of One Lord for all, Who
"per enigmate," allows parallel lines to meet
in His infinity.

Elizabeth Sullam

Customs

(After Frederick Douglass)

My Mother's name was Harriet Bailey.
As was the common custom we were
estranged while I was but an infant.

Did she fashion her raggedy dress
or headwrap from seed sacks? I do
recollect what boots she wore were
tatters from the horses' blankets.

Field slave for a Mister Stewart,
she'd creep twelve miles through
marsh and midnight underbrush
to fold her Little Lamb.

A myriad of moons would pass
between her dark risings first
signaled by the tiniest of taps.
Soon I knew to press lard

around the quarter door,
for if any sound found her,
it might mean the gallows.
Mother lay down beside me,

whispered me to sleep yet
no matter when I'd wake she'd
already stolen away. Providence
granted five such nighttime

visitations. As was common custom
any field hand not at work by
sunrise was horsewhipped until
senseless. Although no slave

can know his birthday, hearsay
may place it at harvest, seed
or snow times. In my seventh
—or eighth—summer and some weeks

past her burial I chanced to hear
of Mother's demise. With no foresight
of my loss or of my life to come
my heart received these tidings as if

learning of a stranger's passing.
Tonight as is my common custom,
I commence my address to the Anti-Slave
Society with the invocation of her name.

And standing before the footlights
of the great auditorium I speak
to all the faces waiting
in the dark. *I do not*

recollect of ever seeing
my mother by the light of day.
My Mother's name was Harriet Bailey.

Chris Llewellyn

The Outing

Before we could go for our Sunday walk
Uncle George had to wash his hands twenty
times. My grandmother and great-grandmother
waited in their lisle stockings and long
sweaters made by loving hands at home.

My great-grandmother wore a sort of mob cap
to protect her hair from bat landings.
We planned to go deep into the woods that day,
beyond the Lincoln-log cabin, coming out
on the other side—of the world, for all I knew.

"George," my grandmother called down the basement
stairs, her voice edged with weariness (fifth call
she'd made). He had lost track of time again—
stacking newspapers on the other side of his room
away from the cruel light. "In a minute, see?"
(He always said *see*, even in the dark.)

My grandmother checked the baskets, rattled the trowels.
Today we would dig up wild ginger pigs with their heart-
shaped leaves and replant them in Mother's rock garden.
"I'm coming, I'm coming," Uncle George shouted through
the pipe he had rigged to relay messages to my grandmother
then came rushing up the steps in his worst straw hat.

But in the time it had taken him to wash his hands,
buckets of rain began to pour down the windows.
He plunged back to the basement for his black umbrella,
but the grannies had taken off their sweaters and sat
by the radio waiting for H.V. Kaltenborn to speak to them.

Shirley Cochrane

Drink

When we got to the spring
I made the customary speech:
whoever drinks this water
will surely return.

And though we both half-knew
you would not be coming back,
you picked a careful path
across damp stones and

buoyed with sudden hope,
put your mouth to the
pipe-mouth buried among
rocks and cress, to the mossy

O and drank. Since then
you have joined the silent
ones beyond all thirst
and hearing. Yet whenever I

bend to the green pipe,
it is you who bend with me
to drink, and you who enter
my mouth as water

rising from the aquifer
of memory to plunge again
into the secret tubes and
vessels of the body.

Jean Nordhaus

After You Died

for Gillian Rudd

After you died
I drove through the dark city
past the silver river
to sit by your bed
I'd heard that the soul
hovers near the body awhile
before beginning its journey
and I remembered how
in the old books
the women washed and anointed
the bodies of those they loved
but, mostly, I had some animal urge
to go to you
not to leave you alone
in your trouble

And though I had no myrrh
nor white linen
to wrap you in
I rubbed lotion on your tired limbs
and wound a white rose
and some baby's-breath
from the windowsill bouquet
through your fingers
Your nails were red and perfect
as always

It was a wet night
No moon or stars
above the invisible trees

The nurse came in and out
We talked
She was good
I'm glad you had a good nurse
the night you died
I wondered if your soul was passing
as your skin grew cool
I was sad
sitting there beside you
just hanging out
the way we always did
even that first month we met
sitting in my courtyard
pulling grass from between the bricks
happy and quiet
talking on and on
two girls
with plenty of life left to live

Mary Ann Larkin

For Neva Maffii Agazzi

We made them ours,
those cities we saw—
side by side on our
daily rides—up
on hills or along main
roads. In Figueroa
we looked at the stunned faces
of Italian workers from Umbria.
Insulted by Dali,
they laughed, "Ma questo scherza."

We would have liked
to stop in every city
which loomed with a spire
on the horizon—a split
in the sky. But we had
to deal with our hurry
to that cemetery in Teruel,
that last city
of the Republican retreat,
and those tombs
with their snakes of ivy,
with all the dead born
after the forties,
and the mass grave.
We shared a La Ina
with that toothless Basque,
the only one left
to remember defeat.

"Come stai?" Your voice
from behind the Atlantic
answers panting, faint
"Non bene..." I try
to think of your loud
voice reciting Martial
in Biblis, but I have
to do the most horrible thing
after our sharing of so many miles:
I have to say good-bye
without sound,
to learn the speech
of the dead before you die.

Elizabeth Sullam

Answer

Forgiveness—that deep forgetting—
if you need it, I can grant it
for I drink glasses of Lethe water
and dine richly on lotus fruit.
Forget, now—*you too*. Whatever
happened was in another time
and in a remote country
    named *home*.

Shirley Cochrane

III

Coming into Being

Invocation

Untether my limbs, sweet mother
Water songs I'll sing
Pond water I'll be
and fall of rain
Moon and stars I'll cradle
on my shimmering breast
Willow wand I'll ride
my flesh now fog and mist
breath of poppies be
sheen of blackbird's wing
No more tramp and plow
Sweet mother, untether me now

Mary Ann Larkin

The Things of the World

I would like to say something for things as they are, in
    themselves,
Not standing for anything else, multiform, legion
In their fleeting exactitude,

Fashioned in intricate and elusive ways, individual,
Each like nothing else precisely. I am speaking
Of observable things, this chair,

This leaf, that slab, the sun, dust, a fly,
Sometimes interacting, sometimes not, depending
On the nature of each, but always

And ever changing, coming into being, vanishing;
May be observed or not; beautiful or ugly
Only as someone's opinion;

Neither right nor wrong; neutral; concerned only with
Their presence here, enduring their given span:
The manifold things of the world.

Robert Sargent

Vision and Revision

I will not voice over
poems written yesterday
or wheedle out of memory
more than is there.
Let each verse howl
as it first comes out
like a child needing
the birth blood
bathed from its eyes
but whose limbs are strong
and already pumping.

Shirley Cochrane

Reappearances

I watch him scrape and smooth,
like an ancient scribe on parchment
gently, painstakingly,
then brush clean the trace
a butterfly left on fossil sand.
Trembling, his hand feels the slight
depression and rests there
as a pilgrim's on a sacred relic.
When he glances up, his eyes,
brilliant with sun's vertigo,
do not see me, but funnel into mine
the flow of ages. Obscurely, my blood
fills the hollow form on stone
and tries to understand itself.

Elizabeth Sullam

Young Man Away from Home

He'd been in the city almost a month, now,
knew no one to talk to,
read books at night in his boarding house bedroom,
had scanned more than once the two letters, one card,
on top of his dresser. Had already written replies.
Restless on a weekend, today he'd taken a bus
to some new unknown place, a part of the city,
gotten off at a random stop,
the two-storied houses set back from the street,
trim lawns, their doors all closed.
Some children were playing hopscotch in one of the yards,
paying him no attention. He walked along, slowly,
arranging words in his head:
    For I have walked down quiet streets where children played,
    where each had to do with himself and himself alone.
Stopped. Scribbled them down in a notebook. Thought,
    not bad.
Walked on. An occasional car, errand intent,
and slow walking strangers, their eyes cast down,
not seeing his glance. Block after block.
And now new words to close things, sum things up:
    And everywhere I looked for one like me,
    and nowhere I found him.
Scribbled down with a smile of triumph. *By God!*
he thought, *not bad. Not bad at all.*

Robert Sargent

Words for Weldon

We haunt ourselves.
              —W.K.

This noon I walked and startled off some crows.
They fell from a knoll—then flew.
                              I thought of you,
Weldon Kees, and how we haunt ourselves
through twilit furnished rooms, at open windows,
in walk-ups we walk up to spectral selves.
Funny:
        the crows did not *caw* today
as ragged winged they leapt and flapped away
with expansive strokes into that taut wind.

It seems I've always heard their tattered song:
the imitable shouts, the gracelessness,
their throats rasping.
                    And lacking your finesse
they nonetheless will sing their big, crude truth—
though not today, as the day you didn't sing,
but flew from the Golden Gate,
                              no word or wing.

Patric Pepper

Sappho

It is so gray in the field of Asphodelus
Stars never shine and the souls
whose rights were denied in life
wander without rest
intangible as air.
The stems of the asphodels
stand still at our passing.
The river dark and silent
runs time and again
around the nether world.

Yet I whom the moon dazzled
and made drunk with silver tones
before seizing me with her light,
walk content among the Shades,
for she freed me from my bond
with the gift of song.
I gave witness to
earth's infinite forms.

I sang utter solitude,
seeking my own kind,
desire for love terse
and cutting as the moon's edge
in those shiny nights
tinged with salt breeze
on the rock of my island
like me a fragment of matter
crumbled by the Gods.

Elizabeth Sullam

The White Meal

Lord, give us food for angels
and invalids, poets and madwomen,
all who find the savor of this world
too strong—mourners and saints
and those volatile souls whose joy
ignites dangerous fevers; for these
a cloud, a polished bone,
a cup of snow is sustenance enough.
Spread them a tablecloth clean

as the page of an unwritten book
and serve upon crockery
plain as a nurse: the clear broth
of memory, skim milk of exile,
cooked grains and potted
cheeses, vegetables culled
from roots of loneliness,
breast-meat, slivered
from the bony tent. Let this feast

be lean as Pharaoh's
seven dream-cows, humble to bless
the blue feet of the starving and let
each vessel, passed from hand to hand
above our plates, inscribe a circle
over circles. Let no clamorous
spice, no storm of seasoning
distract these diners
from their secret craving

to hear a mother's tongue
tolling again in the rooms
of their childhood, watch steam
rising from the early soup,
sunlight flashing from the spoon
raised like a lighthouse
over the sea, a beacon
for the hungry voyager.

Jean Nordhaus

The Klezmer Trio

One WASP pokes the drums, another
Thrums bass fiddle, while a clarinetist
Of indeterminate antecedents cantillates
On his black reed in the nearly dark dive
Where, swaying in shadows, patrons
Ecumenically dance in their chairs as though
They wore earlocks, fringed prayer vests,
Black wide-brimmed hats, as though
Nothing had happened to those other tootlers
Whose music, after all, had not been thought fit
For notice by encyclopedists of music
And is now performed by strangers
For the delectation of strangers.

Edwin Zimmerman

Tin Roof Blues

In the 40's the Condon group made a "Tin Roof Blues"
for once and forever. Brunies was with them that day,
he'd played in the 20's, trombone,
with the New Orleans Rhythm Kings. Think for a moment
how it must have been as they sat around in the studio:
Brunies, Davison, Condon, Russell, Wettling,
Schroeder, and Casey, all for business,
nothing romantic. Condon, let's say, is talking:
"We gotta hold it to five choruses.
Start with the melody, you know," humming. "Now next,
by rights, comes the trumpet, the old Paul Mares solo.
Bill, what d'ye think? You know it, don't you?"
Davison sits there, frowning—it's not
that he doesn't know it—when he plays solo,
he wants it to be his. So Brunies speaks up,
"I'll play it, God, the times I've heard it,
I know it in my sleep." "Wait a minute, George,"
says Condon, "you got to play
your old chorus, that's why we picked this tune.
The one you keep hitting that low B-flat."
"I know," Brunies says. "I'll play Paul's with the mute,
then take it out for mine." "Well, that makes three,"
Condon says. "Then there's that free-for-all.
Can anybody hum it?" Somebody could, and did.
"Then back to the melody," Condon says.
"Slow down on the last four bars. Peewee,
give us a couple of notes to start with. Ready?"
The music begins, swinging slow and full.
What went into it, its perfection,
were simple things, six chords, twelve bars,
and an old New Orleans tune. But mainly
twenty years of learning to do it right.

Robert Sargent

Praise

Great grandmother in dacron brocade suit,
snowflake prayer cap, props her spiral spine
hymnal on the altar rail and raising
her lace hanky, prompts the early arrivers
to join in: "Go tell it on the mountain,
over the hills..." The congregation rises
in response, rolling their rich lyrics
over the double glass storm doors, down
the gravel path of parked cars into
the fallen winter cornstalks.

A stack of tambourines rests on the aisle
end of each white pine pew of the Morning
Star Hill Pentecostal. When the guitar
and piano strike introductory chords,
cousins in bows and cornrows rock
the bench, bat-jingle bat-jingle-bam.
On Daddy's lap, Baby Elizabeth lifts
this instrument in her one-year-old arms,
and with perfect fingers she taps-taps
slowly, slowly, the silver circle bangles.

Chris Llewellyn

Faulkner

With Faulkner, the way he was thought of,
    back home in the 30's:
there'd be four or five people, maybe, sitting around
in somebody's living room, everyone having a drink,
and a cultured, pontifical voice telling us
what we should think of our author. "Of course we know
most of it's trash. Here's a description, though,
of a country road leading down to a nigger's still.
He'd be familiar with that, of course." Titters.
We were being enlightened. "I will say, though,"
reading, "this is a good description. Too bad
there aren't more pearls like this among the filth."
I was the youngest there, held my tongue.

I first read Faulkner in his early books,
not knowing what I was reading.
But late one night, in a third floor hideaway
of Old Lee Hall, I began *The Sound and the Fury*.
I struggled some, at first: "I could see them hitting,"
Caddy becoming Candace. But gradually,
as the night wore on, the campus becoming quiet,
under the yellow lamp, with the turning pages,
I knew that here were people I grew up with,
black and white, the turn of their talk like mine,
the invented, familiar country. Benjy and Jason,
Dilsey, Candace and Quentin, attained their depth,
like Cezanne portraits. Not in France! Here!
And Yoknapatawpha County, as he named it,
not distant like Joyce's Dublin, the Paris of Proust,
but just down the road a piece! It was almost dawn
when I closed the book. I walked back to my room,
across the dark and peaceful campus, exultant.

Of course we can't know exactly how he did it.
But we can speculate.
In Faulkner's study, where *Go Down Moses* was written,
the various tales covering over a hundred years,
with tens of characters, illegal ties of blood,
there *must* have hung on the wall a family tree
of all the McCaslin kinfolk. Now picture Faulkner,
say in an easy chair, ready for work.
Perhaps a glass of whiskey in reaching distance.
He starts to write, then looks up at the chart.
Hmm. I thought that Cass was older than Ike
by 16 years. And Ike born '67.
But this shows Cass born 1850. Still,
could be. A small boy with his uncles. Hmmm.
They'd be about 60 and Cass 9. O.K.
Bends to his writing.

> *When he and Uncle Buck ran back to the house*
> *from discovering that Tomey's Turl had run*
> *again, they heard Uncle Buddy cursing and*
> *bellowing in the kitchen, then the fox....*

Robert Sargent

Emporium Antiques

(Joe Diehl)

Do you recollect his name
—that octogenarian who slept among
cracking volumes of Civil War battles,
who rose only to count
the porcelain tea sets?

Amidst his antique fare, he pointed
to the pageant photo wired
to a plumbing pillar. Had he played
Cro-Magnon? I asked. For there

In long-johns, rabbit-pelt tunic,
he posed beside an isinglass
palm tree. A cotton batting beard
swung down to his groin.

"I portrayed the shepherd
in the Shriners' Nativity."
He pointed out his brother lodgemen.

In still his prime and guru turban,
the town butcher elevated a candy tin
urn. It was the old football coach
who pulled the rope of a wheeled camel.

Swathed in *dishdash* and drawstring
bathrobes, a dozen others genuflected,
facing the wired star. Under its
radiance, an insurance broker Joseph
seemed to be kissing the open palm
of the plaster sleeping infant.

Chris Llewellyn

Trimeters

Exodus 20:11

In closing, let there be trimeters!
Consider the old masters, how they ended their books:
>   *walked back to the hotel in the rain*
>   *each in its ordered place*
>   *yes I said yes I will yes*
with three effortless feet.

And the King James translators in the passage from Exodus,
working on the Fourth Commandment:
"For in six days the Lord made heaven and earth, the sea...,"
did *not* end the phrase with
>   *and all that is in them,*
a piddling dimeter,
but rather a luscious powerful trimeter:
>   *and all that in them is.*

Robert Sargent

IV

In the Company of Writers

The Poetry Group

They sit in a circle in the room
And fuss with one another's words.
They are almost like lawyers
What with their love of specificity,
Their nominal calm while dealing
With grave matters, their calculated
Ambiguities. They could be
Negotiating clauses in a contract
Except that they cock their heads for music,
Except that the business they transact—
In dreams, panging sensibilities, deaths—
Is more elusive than any lawyer's,
And except that they always assume the risk
Of being their own clients.

Edwin Zimmerman

In the Company of Writers

They see with eyes that penetrate their prey
like sun through a magnifying glass.

It's stunning to watch them, in a pack
pounce upon a sickly or injured poem
tearing it verse by verse, stanza by
stanza, reaching into the very center
of a poem, and pulling out its heart
still beating, bleeding.

Sometimes they sit the whole evening
barely making a sound. Only the lights
in their eyes belie their seeming indifference.

Then a lyric, irresistible as the hunter's
moon, possesses them. They lift their heads,
their mouths open and all the beautiful music
of good sense pours out.

It grows warm in the lair with their
affectionate greetings and the communal
feasting of fledgling muses, homemade bread,
fine cheeses, and wine the color of blood.

I've learned not to become too comfortable.
After all, I am in the company of the poetry
police. Nothing personal you understand.
It's just that there are natural laws
that govern poetry and all the universes.

No counterfeit jewelry of prose or fool's gold
of cliché escapes their patrols. I am forced
back to the dark caverns where creativity dwells,
to dig, to dig deeper through the layers of psyche.
That's where the real emeralds, rubies, and diamonds
are found.

It's the scent of fresh language that makes
their mouths water. It's images they crave,
not just to see, but to be transported
to different dimensions, and future landscapes
behind unopened doors.

I love being in this company, especially
when someone brings a particularly
delicate and succulent poetry filet.

They slowly unwrap it. Our hungry eyes
beg for a taste. I realize I have become
one of them. Our tongues do an involuntary
lap around our lips. We devour every
tender word.

Our howls are heard well on into
the deep violet evening.

Keith Yancy

When Keith Comes to Poetry

When Keith comes to poetry group
in his fireman's Blues, a small plug
leading from his left ear, radio
strapped to his waist, his
right ear may be tuned to Mary Ann's
dream of a dying friend
or Patric's poem about the devil
while the other monitors
the city's troubles: crackups
and collisions, ambulance calls,
people stabbed or shot. Perhaps
his father calls him from beyond
death's borders, or he intercepts
the smoldering thought of some
bruised girl-child, or gospel singing
from a sunlit church in Georgia
twenty years ago. When Keith
sits quiet in the tall wing chair
and secret fires play across his face,
we're never sure what frequencies
he hears and whether the voice
will hold flowers or flame.

Jean Nordhaus

V

Watching the City Pass Sideways

Channing Street

What sameness on the street tonight.
The risen moon, like an ancient kite,
Tugs across the starless vault.
The lamps will light to find no fault
With Ebony and her somersault.
The boxcars humble-rumble on
Distantly, and then they're gone
With rusty sides and faded letters.
Here neither side of the track is better.

What humdrum over the twilit street.
Our porches fill in the ebbing heat.
Some teenage boys in baggy pants,
Slow as turtles, quick as ants,
Make of their easy gait cool dance.
And down the block the arithmetic
Of Kara's bike—its perfect click.
The deepening shadows hold no fright;
Oh same, oh same, oh joy tonight.

Patric Pepper

August Days

Now come the August days
Mrs. Sizemore sits on her porch
cuts fruit for the children
The white enamel pan
between her feet
catches the peels and pits
Eat your peach, Joseph, she says
Take your plum, Ebony

Around her
the children fall,
like night flowers
damp with dew
Juices slide unnoticed
down their satin skins
Eat your fruit, children
their mother tells them

Eat your fruit, India and Tiajuana
Take into your bodies, Lynette and Orlando
the sweet pulp your mother prepares for you
Take deep into your sleep-drenched bodies
the silvery pear
the golden peach
the dusky plum
Let the juices fill you
with light enough to keep you
from the soon-arriving dark

Mary Ann Larkin

Kim

(Triplets for a Ward Five waitress)

Swift as wing beats
you dart between
counter and grill.

The blackbirds
on your red shirt not
as jet as netted hair.

Ten egg suns shimmer
easy-over paddy ground
sausage as you turn

down tiny jet flames
spoon up clouds of grits.
Momentarily your head rests

on the microwave and there
closed-eyed and sighing
do you hear the netted heart?

Chris Llewellyn

Junk

On James Hampton's *Throne of the Third Heaven...*
Museum of American Art, Washington, D.C.

Everything begged to be saved:
three-legged tables, arthritic
chairs. The blind lightbulbs
and sprung valises longed to be lifted,
transformed. With his dreaming
eye, he saw them as they might become:
an altar wrapped in foil; the gimpy chair
reborn as throne—though it would not
support a child; six twinned
pedestals with flower-faces
strumming brassy music
of the unreal world. And over all,
emblazoned: *Fear Not.*

The kingdom of heaven is made of junk.
Laboring for years in the dark
garage, he built it, fettling forth
winged symmetries and curious
entablatures, a makeshift architecture,
tenuous as a spider's web.
Transplanted into public view, it leans
toward sleep, still hoarding
its darkness. A velvet ribbon
bars the door to the unenterable room.
You walk away into sorrier streets
than any Hampton could have known.
All is in readiness.

Jean Nordhaus

Arctic

You stepped over the unattended
threshold of a masculine landscape,
all rigor and wind-ablated angles,
distance no horizon line delimits,
no seasons link to rhythms. You face
a never-setting light which radiates
and falls upon itself—realm of silence
and utter solitude. Your Protean mind
adapts in a flash of white and ice—
while your thoughts slip away,
like candid-blue foxes
at the booms of calving ice cliffs.

Elizabeth Sullam

How Many Times Do I Have to Tell Y'all? Delonta Ain't Here!

Two-thirty in the morning they call.
"Is Delonta there? Have you seen Delonta?"

"No, I ain't seen no Delonta."

It's early afternoon now. She can hardly
get anything done in the narrow duplex
mashed between two others just like it.
The cinder block walls are painted pale green.

She is on her knees cleaning out the kitchen
cabinet, the one under the sink, where pots
and pans stand in a tottering tower.

Amid the music of dented tin, they come
knocking. "Is Delonta here?"

"You know what? Y'all about some ignorant
somebodies. I told y'all Delonta ain't here."

A bouquet of plastic flowers, some missing
bulbs, graces a scar-pocked coffee table.
A black belt coils like a snake. A beeper
attached is hissing.

She frowns up her face as if suddenly she
got a whiff of some smelly thing. With one
hand still clutching a pot by its stem
she leans over and shuts the stupid thing off
then goes back to her pots-and-pans music.

A door in the adjoining hallway slowly opens.
A spindly figure in boxers and bow legs
bounces off the door frame while rubbing his eyes.

"Grandma, can you fix me some eggs?"
"Look, Delonta, I ain't nobody's
slave. Fix your own self some eggs."

Keith Yancy

Winter Night

Gun shots: they wake the prudent city dweller,
    whose eyelids snap, knocking the dream aside.
"Checking the piece," one thinks, "or did he kill her
    for love, or pay a debt?" One cannot hide
from the uncontrollable, block upon block
    stretching beyond one's bricked and barred environs,
beyond the blankets, eyelids, and the dark
    blood swishing through the brain.
                        One waits for sirens.
"Will they come?" Oh, yes, wailing official
    compassion, blanking out the city's low,
garrulous murmur. For each boy is special,
    each dreamless one, each one bleeding on snow,
who won't return to sing in church too soon.
    This moment vacant eyes repel the moon.

Patric Pepper

Fall of the Mourning Dove

Lord help us! you mourning doves
are hanging out with pigeons—
did they seduce you with their
coos and flashy iridescence?

Doves, return to your country
meadows with your break-the-heart
calls—who will weep for you
in this break-their-bones city?

Go back to where we left you
even though we may never join you—
we need to know you're waiting
there in your paisley garments

like the fine clothes great-aunts
wear with cultured pearls
and tiny gold earrings made
from Papa's cuff links.

You have a position to uphold—
don't turn into street birds
battling for Popeye thighs
tossed on filthy sidewalks.

Fly now, with your creaking wings
and the whir like a mechanical toy—
flee before you become like the gulls
invading the Metro stations
forgetting the hues of the sea.

Shirley Cochrane

Christmas Morning,
East of the Capitol

The others are all sleeping.
From my desk, I watch the widening
cloud-rows: cirrus and stratus
scribbling messages of light and water
in an alphabet resembling Arabic. Earlier

I went out for milk: tiny stars
in plate glass windows blinking, racks
of bread arrayed in breathing rows,
in lighted cases, the dairy products
stunned as figures in a diorama.

Merry Christmas. Merry Christmas,
the Korean grocer murmurs—
far from home, his labor
never ends. *Leisure and pleasure,*
Hannah said last night at dinner,

that's what art is for. And Ted—
they love to argue—*Everything
can be art, even a speech, a paper.*
I say *amen* to all work done
with love and in obedience

to its own necessity. Now the rows
of cloudscript open into ribs
of a heavenly scrubboard, and as I lift
my pen to write, seagulls, wheeling
south, begin the new day's washing.

Jean Nordhaus

Graffiti as a Sure Testament to Love

On an overpass of the Southwest Freeway
a fading message reads:
ROBERT & CLAUDIA
PARTY ANIMALS IN LOVE
and this one, on a bridge in Georgetown:
ROBERT & CLAUDIA
TOGETHER FOREVER

Over the years I've thought
about Robert and Claudia
those aging party animals
their old signs bleaching out.
Still together? Living
in a split-level house
with their two and a quarter kids? Or did they split
up, say in 1979, because
the thrill was, you know,
gone?

But wait!
Just yesterday on a slung-up fence
at 12th and F Northwest appeared
ROBERT & CLAUDIA
PARTY ANIMALS
IN FATUATION
as persistent as Kilroy,
these two, still here
beginning all over again.

Shirley Cochrane

The Legend

He and his horn have flown first class
to clubs in Paris, Tokyo, Nairobi, and New York.

Tonight, he stood under the exposing spotlight
in a small club, hidden in an alley somewhere
in Georgetown, bombed out of his mind.

His head fell forward, mouth hung open
as if this would focus the blurred picture
before his eyes.

With a shrug that said "so what," he lowered
his head a little further, and on the first try
found the tip of the tenor saxophone floating
in space.

The first lush tones of a ballad circulated
through the cramped tables and chairs
like an island breeze. We leaned back,
stretched our legs as the tiny club seemed
to grow larger.

His back arched when the set turned up-tempo.
The horn like some ancient alchemist's oven
transformed his heated breath to liquid fire.

When his solo should have ended, he kept playing.
Searing notes erupted from the big brass crater
and spread across the wooden sky, vented through
the blown-out walls

flowed in torrents down the narrow ravine
of the alley, and poured over the steep cobblestones
of Wisconsin Avenue towards the river, lying stagnant
and satisfied with its muddiness.

When the scorching mass of notes tumbled into
the startled river, it pulsated with awakened
spray and once again craved the salt of the sea.
And we understood why he is a legend and why
we forgave him.

Keith Yancy

The Cairo Hotel

(A pillow-art by Joanna Pessa)

Stuffed silver pillow portrays
the massive carved entryway,
inverted bow shows art nouveau
letters: C - A - I - R - O.

Before red lining or gentrification,
hotel inhabitants lined the etched
palm archways, sat in oases
of folding chairs to hold court,
newspapers, and paper bag wineskins.

During Diaspora, these old pharaohs
and sibyls turned into bedouins,
winding their cloaked wanderings
up Seventeenth Street, spelling
their secrets-of-the-ages through
the red-letter aisles of Safeway
and preaching prophecy beneath
the golden arches of McDonald's.

After Evacuation, a sandstorm machine
blasted clean, leaving the gargoyle
spouts and filigree spotless
for the new gods ascending
silver-stuffed on the horizon.

Portending winter, some pilgrims
turned to stone. One pillowed
her head on a step, slept bowed
in plastic bags, only an alley
cat sphinx keeping vigil.

Chris Llewellyn

The Route of Eli Washington

Congress Heights is Eli Washington's bus
and he doesn't pay one cent of fare, nor
does the driver stop him. He wears green
Army fatigues, brogans, and a hat like those
used as sunshades for mules; and mules
is what Eli smells of on this July night:
mules and loam and fires long burned out.

The librarian he chooses as seatmate
makes a nose-bandage of her hand
and breathes sideways, glancing
at the paper napkin on his wrist
secured by three rubber bands.
Women on the bus won't talk to him
though he calls them ladies
and wants to inform them of his life.
"I own the U.S. Treasury," he says,
"but there ain't no money in it."
And for all we know, he may be right.
He owns the Hyatt-Regency too,
"But they won't let me sleep there."

He asks a question of the woman
in the purple dress (too hot for July);
she turns great El Greco eyes upon him
and says *si*, for which he thanks her.
An older woman, edema-swollen flesh
under white lisle hose, gives him
a wife-look, sad and disgusted:
Suppose you had to take this
man into *your* bed? He rises,
goes to sit on the step close
to the driver. He says to no one
in particular but to anyone listening,

"If I didn't love you so much,
I would kill you dead." It's
then that we notice in his hip
pocket, the knife, tip pointing
toward heaven and an uncertain death.
Watching the city pass sideways,
he says: "My God, my God,
what have they done to my city?"

Shirley Cochrane

Alley

Bobbing the leaves like August's moody ghost,
    the wind, seen only as effect,
enamels soot to each unmoving host,
       every sill and deck,
and lightly peppers now the sheds and cars
       with gritty stars.

Mrs. Cheatham's cats do flits and turns;
    her bulging peaches blaze through leaves
and line the limbs, as her house, each brick, burns
       with mortal sun that sleeves
in plain and ancient light the present day
       as yesterday.

The starlings and the sparrows flutter down
    the azure skirt of heaven; squirrels
acrobat across a power line;
       the empty, airy curls
of pearly sheets hung out last night to dry
       drift in the eye.

And then the car pool blares, the factory's trumpet
    declaring this the day and now
the time to roar for work, to heave and hump it.
       Reluctantly we stand now,
though everything abides, each day, right here,
       without us near.

Alleluia! Striped and orange alley
    cats and collard greens like wings,
all day today the languid dillydally
       of The Ten Thousand Things,
our nameless alley sings, *Alleluia!*
       Alleluia!

Patric Pepper

A Good Day in a Bad Neighborhood

Spring had come early. Even the gray
streets responded, trying to shake
off the layers of salt and dust.

A carnival was underway in the shabby
brick stores stuck together in a row.
They blinked their iron-barred eyes
in the hybrid sunlight.

Doing steady trade, three dollars
at a time. A pack of cigarettes
a beer and a pickle, a bag of chips
a loaf of bread, a can of mackerel.

Shorts in pneumonia weather and drab
legs marched up the afternoon hill
and sat on stoops that winter had
recently occupied.

You could hear the music of shining
cars that flew too fast, like jacamar
and toucan birds trying to attract
a mate.

Hungry kids in dingy tops traveled
in a pack singing the latest hits
and lifting their long arms into
the air swollen with pollen and dogwood
making it across the neglected asphalt
just ahead of oncoming traffic.

You could almost smell the lotus
and mango trees. It was as if
something had broken free after being
held back for so long.

The goddess of hope had briefly
and accidentally made her way here.

Keith Yancy

Orion Blesses Ward 5

It was his belt that I saw first
winking above the back alleys
For years he had abandoned me
Now he'd come back
loose and free above this house
of light and sorrow
these sore sleeping alleys
the bruised tenderness of Ward 5
He came in the pre-dawn dark
in the southern sky, of course,
in the autumnal sky
as if above a seaside cottage
or a country pond
Reaching through years
of leavings and findings
he spills his blessings over us
gathers us up
in his long starry arms

Mary Ann Larkin

BIOGRAPHIES

SHIRLEY COCHRANE, who teaches at Georgetown University's School of Continuing Education and at The Writer's Center, is the author of two books of poems: *Burnsite* (Washington Writers' Publishing House) and *Family & Other Strangers* (Word Works). A manuscript entitled *Letters to the Quick/Letters to the Dead*, is scheduled for 1997 publication by Signal Books in her home state of North Carolina. She has recently recorded her poems for the Library of Congress poetry archive. She is a founding member of the Capitol Hill Poetry Group.

Individual poems have appeared most recently in *International Poetry Review, Poet Lore*, and *The Cape Rock*. Other poems have been anthologized, including poems in two books of the Harry Abrams' art and poetry series. She is also a fiction writer.

MARY ANN LARKIN is a poet, teacher, writer, and former development consultant, who presently teaches English at Howard University. Her poetry has appeared in many literary magazines such as *New Letters* and *Antietam Review* and in anthologies such as *America in Poetry* and *Loving,* (Harry Abrams). Her first book was *The Coil of the Skin* (Washington Writers' Publishing House), followed by *White Clapboard* (Carol O. Allen).

CHRIS LLEWELLYN has taught poetry workshops in elementary schools, colleges, prisons, and for adults and children at The Writer's Center in Bethesda, MD. She has been published in dozens of anthologies and periodicals and has received numerous awards, among which are the Walt Whitman Award from the Academy of American Poets and the Fellowship in Creative Writing from the National Endowment for the Arts. Since 1994 she has served as an instructor of creative writing in AmeriCorps/WritersCorps.

JEAN NORDHAUS has served as President of Washington Writers' Publishing House and Coordinator of Poetry Programs at the Folger Shakespeare Library. Her second book of poems, *My Life in Hiding*, appeared in *Quarterly Review of Literature* in 1991. She is a founding member of the Capitol Hill Poetry Group.

PATRIC PEPPER is a manufacturing engineering manager living in Washington, D.C. His work has appeared in *Hungry as We Are: An Anthology of Washington Area Poets*, and in periodicals such as *The Hiram Poetry Review*, *Poetpourri*, and *Hellas*. He received Honorable Mention in the 1993 Chester H. Jones Foundation National Poetry Competition.

ROBERT SARGENT'S fifth book of poems was *The Cartographer* (Forest Woods Media Productions). His previous books are *Now Is Always the Miraculous Time, A Woman from Memphis, Aspects of a Southern Story*, and *Fish Galore*. He is a longtime member of the Washington, D.C. poetry community. He was awarded the 1996 Merit Award, given by the Folger-based Poetry Committee for the Greater Washington Area, for the support of poetry.

ELIZABETH SULLAM'S first novel of historical fiction, *A Canossa*, was recently published by Camunia Publishing House in Italy. A book of poems, *Out of Bounds*, was published by Catholic University of America in 1987. She was born in Italy and now lives and works in the U.S. Her poems have appeared in *Poets for AIDS* and other anthologies and journals.

KEITH YANCY is a native Washingtonian. He has been a member of the D.C. Fire Department for the past 23 years and currently holds the position of lieutenant. Keith worked as a music programmer and engineer during the early years of radio station WPFW. His work has appeared in *Obsidian II, The African American Review, The Griot,* and *Sons of Lovers,* an anthology by Oyster Knife Publishing. He is a member of the African American Writer's Guild.

EDWIN ZIMMERMAN is a Washington attorney. He has had a lifelong interest in poetry and is a member of the Folger Poetry Board.